my heart became a bomb

emerging voices from the middle east


Series Editor
*Dena Afrasiabi*


Other titles in this series include:
*Dying in a Mother Tongue*
*Using Life*
*Limbo Beirut*

# my heart became a bomb

Poems by
RAMY AL-ASHEQ

*Translated from the Arabic by*
DINA ABOUL HOSN, NIDA AWINE AND LEVI THOMPSON

*Edited by*
LEVI THOMPSON

Cover Artwork by Akil Ahmad
Cover Design by Ramy Al-Asheq
Book Design by Allen Griffith of Eye 4 Design

Library of Congress Control Number: 2020950267

# contents

my heart became a bomb

# introduction

You have in your hands the debut of Ramy Al-Asheq's poetry in English, translated from the Arabic. A Syro-Palestinian born in 1989 in Sharjah, in the United Arab Emirates, Ramy grew up in the Yarmouk Camp for Palestinian refugees in Damascus, Syria. Following the outbreak of the Syrian revolution in 2011, he worked as a journalist in Syria and wrote revolutionary poetry and song lyrics until Bashar al-Assad's regime arrested and imprisoned him. After his release, regime sympathizers harassed him, forcing him into hiding for nine months. He then made his way to Jordan where he was again arrested and held in the Cyber City prison camp for Palestinians fleeing Syria, located near the northern city of Irbid. He eventually escaped and went into hiding for over two years in the Jordanian capital, Amman, where he published his first book in Arabic, *Walking on Dreams*, a collection of poems about the uprising in Syria. From there, Ramy earned a writing fellowship from the Heinrich Böll Foundation, which brought him to Cologne, Germany in 2014, where he took up residence in the Nobel laureate's house. Ramy has since published widely in Arabic and in German translation and has been a regular participant in the German art scene, providing poetry for several exhibitions and art installations. A collection of Ramy's poetry in Arabic, called *The Dogs of Memory*, was published in a German translation undertaken by Lilian Pithan in 2019, under the title

1

*Gedächtnishunde.* Most recently his 2016 collection of prose texts, titled *Ever Since I Did Not Die*, translated by Isis Nusair, appeared in English in late 2020.

I have been corresponding with Ramy for several years as one of his English translators. The poems that follow, then, are the product of a long collaboration that has taken place over e-mail and direct messages between myself and the poet. Although Ramy and I have never met in person, we have had a close working relationship, the sinews of which are held together digitally. I am fortunate to have been able to ask his opinions about the English translations of his poems. But I am not the only translator involved in bringing these poems to English. Dina Aboul Hosn translated "No One Noticed When You Died," and Nida Awine translated "From Within," "Three Attempts To Say I Love You," "At War," "The War Is Lucky," and "Pictures From Exile" before I began translating the other poems. Their work has informed my own. As editor of the collection, I have attempted to give the poetic voice some coherence, and to that end I have in some cases introduced changes to my collaborators' translations. Any faults that remain in the English versions are, therefore, mine alone, and I thank my collaborators, Ramy, and Dena Afrasiabi, editor of the series Emerging Voices from the Middle East at UT Austin's Center for Middle Eastern Studies, for the opportunity to put these poems together in this edition.

*My Heart Became A Bomb* brings Ramy's harrowing story of war, imprisonment, and escape to English readers in a timely collection. The English translations retain the direct and compelling free-form structure of the original Arabic poems. Moreover, by refusing to offer our personal interpretations of the original Arabic and its often enigmatic resonances, the English translators allow the verse to frequently preserve its mysterious quality as the poems flow from one image to another. Throughout the collection, readers will find themselves here on battlefields amidst the debris of war, there on boats overcrowded with refugees in the Mediterranean. Ramy's revolutionary voice offers more questions than it does answers, challenging God in the wake of war, "Hey Allah! / If you were a man . . . I'd kill you!"

So ends the last poem of this collection, "No. 2935." Written during a journey Ramy took to the Auschwitz concentration camp in 2017, the poem imagines a conversation between the poetic persona and a Holocaust victim (or witness—the character remains ambiguous) in a lament for the passing of the civil engineering student Rihab al-Alawi, who was tortured to death by prison guards in a Syrian jail in 2013. The poems leading up to this offer little respite from the continuing violence in Syria. "From Within" challenges representations of the war in Europe while foregrounding the experience of forced migration to a wholly new land. The speaker of "In The Wide Arms Of War," declaims to a European interlocutor, "we take off fear like a shoe with an open mouth, / run around barefoot, / and smile / for the photo to be less terrifying for your European friends." "No One Noticed When You Died" investigates the power of remembrance, of origin, against a backdrop of violence. "We modeled our memories into missiles. / How many might they kill?" In "Three Attempts To Say I Love You," the poetic persona tries to hold off time and death as he reflects on the relationship between deed and intention, drawing on a well-known saying of the Prophet Muhammad. "At War" seeks a poetic beginning in the horrors of war and provides the title of the collection when it declares, "War doesn't know that death fashions poets. / As for me . . . Death grips the waist of my song, / and my heart, / my heart became a bomb." The next poem, "The War Is Lucky," is a difficult reflection on living through war. It asks what might have happened to misdirect a bomb intended for the poet. "It could be that / the pilot mistook the type of bomb / or left me alone on purpose. / Perhaps a black hand landed on his own / and pulled the trigger. / Perhaps his phone rang, and he throttled down. / Perhaps a fragment of my luck played out the last part / of the story." The long poem "Fatma Carries Two Wounds In One Hand" and the shorter "In The Sea's Playground" tell the stories of migrants at sea.

The first is a long reflection on a mother's journey across the waters to a new country and the second a pithy presentation of the sea, death, and revenge. Several other poems looking back across the sea onto swirling memories of a troubled past round out the collection.

Overall, Ramy's poetry challenges standard definitions of what makes a poem a poem in Arabic. While rhyme and rhythm play some formal part in the original Arabic poems, Ramy eschews many of the metrical rules that Arab poets have retained for more than a thousand years. Yet, I would hesitate to call the poems collected here prose poetry, a genre that also exists in Arabic. Instead, Ramy's playful use of form reflects his poetic persona's defiance of Arabic's poetic past. For example, in "What Dark Wants," the penultimate poem of the collection, the persona's complaints make sense only once we have situated the poem within the Arabic poetic tradition, a tradition that remains closely linked with Islam. "Everyone writes that he's like a moth / around the flame of its beloved," the persona grumbles. This is a reference to a common trope in mystical poetry in Islam, the poetry of the Sufis, in which the lover (the moth, the poet) circles the flame of the beloved (the candle, the Beloved, the Divine). Ramy's persona here reacts to this trope and rejects it. "Before I give the poem something to say, / I have to kill all the moths just in case. / If I can't, I'll have to eliminate the word / 'moth' from the dictionary, / if I can't . . . / I'll burn the old poetry along with the new / and go into seclusion . . . ." In the end, the persona must react to the weight of the Arabic poetic tradition in the same way that it responds to persistent memories of trauma, war, and exile. This poetic stance thus ties the collection together thematically. If we have been able to carry this theme over for you, the reader, the English translation will have been a success.

Levi Thompson
*Providence, Rhode Island*
*18 Nov. 2020*

# from within

*Translated by Nida Awine*

When we set off for war
you, wearing all new clothes,
and I, carrying a pierced heart,
we had to part.
The war desires me alone . . .

Borders defined by others
spread their legs,
Other others came in,
violating my mouth,
forcing me to look in their eyes
to see myself without teeth
or country.

When we set off for war
I held your hand,
and satellites watched us,
so we shed the cold

to tell the other side of the world,
"Don't worry,
for we have yet to reach your borders!"

Like an unknown village in India,
we had names and election tickets
valid for museums
and film awards —
actors posed in photos with us,
smiling,
before washing themselves a dozen times
to get out the stink of our sorrow.

When we set off for war . . .
God entered into the sniper's barrel,
like a genie returning to his lamp
from the impossible mission of granting three wishes,
three wishes I couldn't know less about.

A shell fell by accident,
a teenage girl's diary flew away and burned up,
a tattered page survived bearing the words,
"We don't want you to feel guilty tomorrow.
We just want you to keep the holocaust from winning."
It stayed there, hanging between sky and flame.

My hand, cracked by sadness,
tried to be a merciful sea
for murderers to cross and wash themselves.

Your delicious face,
like the last piece of bread in a siege,
burned up and fell down
from longing.

When we went out for a stroll with war,
on a sleepless tank's penis,
the blood of dreams streamed down.

My father was neither an informant nor a military man,
neither poet nor revolutionary.
He was normal,
like any dictator.

The Damascene woman,
who was washing the stink of soldiers
from her threshold's memory,
suffocated
from abandonment.

When we set off for war,
friends were flying and falling down
like spring flowers.
I was a tire, burning to block the path
of a plane.
You were a bird migrating to a country
that does not understand the language of its chirps.

We set off for war,
without windows to carry so we could watch ourselves
from them.

We carried mirrors
that we see your children's faces in.
You, who are waiting to celebrate the end of the war
without putting a single bullet in its head.

If only the war knew who it kills,
it would become the queen of gods.

I will not tell you about blood.
I will open a pack of cigarettes,
hold a stone from a ruined city,
and throw it in the pond;
if it becomes colorful,
I will set it aside
and then throw another one,
and so on . . .
until I build you a poem.
People will ask
"Why did you forget to add rhythm and rhyme?"
Forget it.
They don't know that the music of war
has no rhythm,
and that we are rhymes
sharing the same ending without an opportunity to sing.

There you are,
far away from bombs.
Fear resounds like thunder
here.
In the wide arms of war,
we take off fear like a shoe with an open mouth,

run around barefoot,
and smile
for the photo to be less terrifying for your European friends.
We send the pictures by snail mail
to escape the censors who care more for animals
than for anyone without the right passport.
We write on them,
"Sorry we can't send video clips . . .
the worst thing about war is
that it makes noise when it eats."

# no one noticed when you died

*Translated by Dina Aboul Hosn*

No one noticed when you died.
You had delegated devastation,
and your devastation delegated us.
And then you rested . . .
No one noticed when you died.
Are you gone?

Everyone knew about your death—
they all noticed,
they ignored you and carried on,
they proposed a thousand toasts for your death.
In honor of your death—
they ignored you and carried on.

They painted your face
a thousand times on the wall
and carried on.

They wrote, in handwriting that looked like yours,
what they wanted.
They divided your land amongst themselves
and returned.

"How many times have we betrayed you?" they asked,
and they carried on.
The sun knows all of us . . .
How did they get through?
Have they ever uncovered one of the cowardly sun's sins,
the ones they told each other about?
The ones they used to twist the sun's injured arm,
declaring,
"That's a secret!"

As we get on in years,
we forget more of the tale.
How long has it been?
Time doesn't know,
and the timekeeper can't judge.

We become weaker,
the stronger our yearning gets.
Whenever the call to prayer sounds,
and as the years go by,
the weaker we become . . .

As we become weaker, we get more violent . . .
We walk to find out who it is that moves us,
and we fall.
Who moves us?

Do you know?
If you do,
then how could you utter a single syllable after this death?

We become weaker
whenever they invent a weapon,
whenever a fighter asks a question, then rests
Whenever a teacher reads something in God's book
about a brazen death.

And you, you left.
I can almost feel your pain.
Are you relieved?
You asked for death.
You screamed.
You died several times,
and you lived.
I don't know what death looks like,
but they say that death lies at the end of wasting away.
I sealed up death with wax,
I waited for my ending,
I counted my dead.
I've just noticed the dead and the living.
Who sows the seeds of night in the fields of day?
"Me!"

I got used to waiting to leave with a question,
and I have not arrived.
I am a powerless god
who abandoned guardianship and rested
on a question.

I wonder
who moves all this death?
I doze off
and wake up—
"Who will repair everything I laid waste to?"
I ask.
Who will answer me?
"Death does it!"
"Then what?"
"Only Death knows."
I'm not concerned with answering the perennial question.
My real concern
is to find an answer
that doesn't cause any harm.


"How many times have we betrayed you?" they asked
before they carried on.


Nothing knows us
We travel. We don't travel.
We carry on
and never arrive.
Mirrors seem to renounce us,
and we modeled our memories into missiles.
How many might they kill?
How many might survive?
The only thing the newborn inherited is the truth of the stories.
How do we know ourselves?
To tell the truth, we are mutants—

Do we deny our origin?
Prophets about to weep from accusations . . .

We believed in superstition
and triumphed.
We embraced a singer's *falsetto*,
we magnified the crime,
delegating God as a sword
to fight with wishes.

God is a monster
in the minds of the scared,
as they drag their chains,
while God remains free . . .

"How many times have we betrayed you?" they asked
before they carried on.

God appears in cigarette smoke.
I am the smoke.
I see him in myself.
I pass away,
yet I don't see God rebel.
I'm still asking people to fight my war
so that bullets will cover me up.

The fire is my fire . . .
and the land—paradise—experienced my destruction.
How do I survive the siege?

How does God survive drunk concubines?
Does He travel?

The war is my war
Blood has taken over paradise,
mixing with entrails,
and the land of others has triumphed
—without me—
Will I be defeated?
I'm already defeated,
but my destruction cannot uncover me.

Every girl who rests
in my bed
increases the number of cannons.
All the sounds of my rape
urge me
to put up a defense . . .
I got old while death stayed
young.

I fear flowing.
Anything that flows like a river
could not flow from me.
Every poem,
every love,
every revolution . . .
And revelation . . . Whoever threw revelation into our heads,
is just a senile man who wants the throne
to himself.

I was the only one who said,
"Revelation is a disgrace."

I fear flowing
for no reason
other than the river gives no opportunity for
the story
to turn into wine.

# three attempts to say i love you

*Translated by Nida Awine*

1      "I love you," she said
Then a little girl got lost pulling back the clock hands.
We reckoned the squadron of planes was still far off,
so we got closer,
and the planes
knew that gravity made our ancestors' apple fall
from the same sky.
At that moment the black apple did not know
how to make its break, how to explode.


2      "I love you," she said.
A prison guard went by,
and she fell asleep.
The hallway: a path to our quick gasp for air,
two iron panels between us,
two faces waiting for the path to be free of nonexistence.

"I love you," she said.
I didn't answer
I didn't find her
I didn't sleep!


3     "I love you," she said.
But death
kept me from chasing lips for a while.
I intended to say goodbye to this ugly universe
in an embrace like this.

I intended to reconcile with all the hours of refuge.
In fact, I only said hours so my twenty years wouldn't
become two million,
in case I forget, afterwards,
how I could have colored my blackness if I'd known love before.

I intended to
bring back the story of the apple in the industrial age.
"Who seduces whom?"
All the spy equipment will reveal our mystery.
I didn't know
that something might reveal it
if the prophecy were fulfilled,
if I could go back to the beloved past,
if justice could heal the wound in my neck.
I will seek out a great death once more
to know the final mystery, to know the end.

How I had intended
to distribute refugees there
in the absurdity of diaspora,
colored in without the features of refugees,
without any music in their language to expose them,
without memories in the back of their minds
pulling them lower and lower
to give the poem its daily due.
I intended to give my little ones the craft of dreams
in ruined dungeons
to teach them all
—even though I hate kids—
the sounds of women across the bed,
that women are a beautiful homeland,
that devotion is an absolute love for beauty
not for homelands!
For them to have a thousand identities, residences,
and documents,
To bear, in every capital, a child.
Those who hide women from the air are not countries . . .
I want an entire army, colored with bad temper.

I intend,
I had intended,
To tell her, "I love you"
—a second ago—
To climb towards her eyes
and plant a kiss that would not fade
"People shall know women by their eyes."

and I intended
to watch her silence and bewilderment,
the numbness of lips on lips.
Rivers of sweat
when they merge in victory are a toast to the salt of our fires,
the lust of music
when wine runs out in the cellars' breaths . . .
I intended
to tell her the truth
I cannot be faithful.
An army of children is forcing me to live without a homeland

I really did intend
to tell her the whole truth.
I even intended to add,
"Deeds have nothing to do with intention."[2]

Cologne 2015

---

[2] This line is in reference to a *hadith*, a saying attributed to Muhammad, the Prophet of Islam, which goes, "The reward of deeds depends upon intentions, and every person will receive rewards according to what he has intended."

# at war

*Translated by Nida Awine*

At war, I give you weapons,
so give me your blood.
The sky is closing in.
Fear has colored your bloody breast,
and your face floods with fire and gunpowder.
Your hand waves.
My hand kisses your Damascene color.
The bullets ask me,
"Aren't you scared?"
"Yes," I say and shoot off a round from my broken eyelid,
purely for your face,
"Burn, O Lover! The cold is bluer than your lips,
and the fire asks you to stay."

Blood . . .
and your face floods with silence and water.
Calm is your remaining question.
Your darkness is lit with oil.
The world is illuminating darkness
at war.

What do I have,
except your face in ruins?
I carried weapons, but I got scared!
I wrote poetry; it broke off at the end.
I said, "Let destruction stay until the day I meet you."
It finished me off,
and longing could not manage longing,
and I was alone in battles that never were.

At war
I give you the poem.
Give me a pen, like an eyelash an eyelid
could no longer contain
fallen suicidal on the body of a book.
Take my hand,
and give me your last kiss in the morning
without me knowing it
without you throwing your shadow across my body.
Don't tell me, "Goodbye, I'm his now."
Ignore him!
Silence the intuition of women.
This is how death dies, furious in the dark.
Death knows its Achilles' heel.

At war
birds are not strong enough to sing.
I saw a bird shit on a soldier,
I saw an ostrich get up with an angry head,
I saw a plane with no voice stare at children so they disappeared.
At war bullets flow out of eyes

But when I am at war,
my shoes eat me like a little tyrant
eats his house.
If I'm wounded I take them off,
so why did my wound startle them?

My foot is walking backwards
Longing reached its rival,
walked up to him and put him in cuffs.

At war absence begs, "Take me, my son."
I pay no attention to him,
then I quote the question, and I disappear to ask him.

I live like the last of the dead,
taking the mirage in his hands to deliver it.

At war I experience life and life's death.
My face, as if dust is its amulet.
Death completes me,
and my death completes it.

At war, time doesn't stop
at the checkpoints of the siege.
I walk with cut-off hands, and my face is a flame-thrower,
angry like a tank.
At war I can be a massacre all by myself.

One day, I'll dwell on your bloody face
and count all the disappointments of life.

I trace the end
Like the one who flipped the book over to interpret it,
trace salvation,
and hurry it along.

O Murderer . . .

War doesn't know that death fashions poets.
As for me . . . Death grips the waist of my song,
and my heart,
my heart became a bomb.

# the war is lucky

*Translated by* Nida Awine

The war is lucky
that I didn't say what happened . . .

My face, and the bullet,
for example, I didn't say,
"I lost my suitcase!"
My eyes are two planes fleeing from the country's colors
to the color of her eyes.
All this earth is flour
that bakes us.
Kids pull grief out of dust.
A doll that
didn't survive—neither did its owners—a trip pointing to the sky,
a trip that was only

Blood
unseen,
salt, shadows, stones,
a hand patting the shoulder of a projectile that failed
to paint the place,

a funeral that never made it to the gravedigger,
a plane that sifts through things, then gives us documents for life
a girl was running to see him, and he didn't come!
A hand counts waving fingers
then dissolves into asphalt.
Taverns drench their tiles with wine, to forget.

At night,
between the dead and the dead,
I asked the ashes of our house about old photos.
How can I prove that I was once blond?
That I was a child once somewhere?
I asked the shadows of our house about the little bell, its ring,
and the strange name for a stranger: my father.
I asked myself,
in light of the curiosity of those who thought it was an alias,
about windows looking out over the dead on the way
to the cemetery.

Again I ask
about those living in a chest drawer
and the conversations that were missing from the music
of the end,
about the doorknob that fell and stayed there,
wood and a peephole.
The magic of the story couldn't stay
between "what I may have been" and the truth.
Any documentation of the story was lost.
Perhaps time has given up on sin.
I had different eyes.
The skies would say, "Their memory is our home."

I had no poems or countries
I was . . .
I was . . .
But I didn't know the truth, that there's no past without pictures;
I asked the ruins of our house,
"How did people used to celebrate a memory?"
A piece of ceiling answered by falling down on me,
but I survived and
danced triumphantly in the grim reaper's disappointed face!

I left that place,
stole someone's wallet that had two ripped
up pictures, one of him and another of oblivion
drowned in sand.
The blood tells me,
"Between noon and night, a face lit up in the distance requests,
'Kiss me . . .'"
So he kissed the picture of oblivion
and the place broke apart . . .

For him and for oblivion, for the poor pictures,
for faces absent from the place,
for two pictures preserving the autumn of love,
for the time and salt of a family that appeals ignore . . .
The photographer didn't date them.
For clothes tossed out for others in the hopes of a meeting,
for meeting,
for faces smiling at mirrors while waiting for a gift,
for the flame when it overlooks the fire
for her Majesty's fear of the rabid ruler's dogs
for forgetfulness, remembrance,

for staring at the deceased through his creator's eye,
and for God who in his destroyed house,
for me . . .
for us, the dead and the living,
I didn't tell the truth.

I didn't say I survived
because I didn't.
But I also didn't die.

A disruption in missile distribution
wanted me alive and
lonely like this war.
Surrounded by my body parts,
no one curses me like a war!

I looked at a place that was here before the superstition
of short time,
and I found an explanation there.
It could be that
the pilot mistook the type of bomb
or left me alone on purpose.
Perhaps a black hand landed on his own
and pulled the trigger.
Perhaps his phone rang, and he throttled down.
Perhaps a fragment of my luck played out the last part
of the story.
Maybe he didn't know me,
or perhaps he did.
I was distracted.
Maybe a bird flew by and saved me,

saving himself from all the complexity of life.
Maybe the place launched itself around for me
to stay alive or to travel.
Not place, not me
not home
not the pilot
not the sound of the bomb
not the bomb shell
not the suitcase
not the wall
not the shadows
not the music
not the hand, the paint, the wardrobe, the windows,
the cemetery, our name,
not the home
not the old photos
No one!
We were all together in space and time,
and we never were.

So, it's a good thing
my poem was written at my leisure.
I survived just like it did,
and it's bad luck for the war
that I didn't die!

# fatma carries two wounds in one hand

*Translated by Levi Thompson*

**1**         **a cross section of memory**

"The sea is white"
she said, the bride on the path.
She thinks
the water is weaker than the two marriages that have followed
me all my life!
I used to think about
her teaching me how to swim.
How? I don't know, but I recall
that she would ruthlessly throw my heart
into the sea, not fearing Pharaoh, no,
but in search of a prophet.
I recall that she
would float as if she were the mother of the waves
to protect the waters from evaporation.
She was the first, like all mothers,
to ward off the waters,
to hide what she could of her femininity,
and dive into the sea still wearing her clothes and veil

2       **a marginal note**

Fatma
fears politics, but not the seas.
She circulates through the police stations
giving every policeman a little mothering.
She opens an old photo album to soften his heart,
so she can find out where her son is.


3       **another cross section of memory**

She tried to teach me to sit still
but she couldn't!
She would organize my songs every week
and arrange my toys.
I was a crazy kid
my playground haste, tears,
and bawling.
That's over now.
It was to my benefit,
and perhaps
the crying subsided as a delayed yet urgent response to
something.


4       **mother of the poem**

Fatma prepares the ship for me.
Shall I prepare my waiting for her?
O Mother of the Poem, how can patience
bring about your defeat and mine?

5 **weaning**

Fatma
will open her chest to the sea
to suckle it, to remain steadfast.
She knows all this salt
she knows how to sprinkle it on food
and how to wean her child.

6 **a veil**

Fatma
will bare her head to the sea.
I know she recited poetry and the Quran to it,
and she smiled at the water's face.
She pretended to be dizzy, spreading out her body
face to face with the sunrays
face to face with a deceitful sky.
She wants to keep it wide,
to see the deceit
clearly as she looks out,
and the sea
betrays swimmers just as it betrays scent!

7 **recalibration**

The sea has a capital city and fire.
O Old Sea, come on, let's make a deal—
The sea can have whatever craziness wants,
and I'll take her youth.
O Sea, I bequeath you tranquility.

I am the son of Acre.
Memories of the water might be useful,
so don't ever be her sky.
Be peaceful.
We are the ones who tamed your waves
morning and night
in reality and beyond!

8    **a boat**

Fatma binds herself up in her craving.
The boat overflows with pilgrims,
the sun is their *qiblah*
and the sea their prayer rug,
unfit for ablutions.
The sea has become memories of those who drowned
and the mirror of the sky.
God's throne has disappeared from the sea
and beyond,
but Fatma's face hasn't disappeared.

9    **heavy with milk**

Fatma prepares the garden for us, and the milk,
as if we
were not able to make the seas less wavy
and the sky lighter.

10 **waiting for a miracle**

Fatma,
O Mother of Truth,
how many times we lied to see you.
How many times we lied
to hide our faces
from the fire of your fear.
The time has come for the seas to rise up to your hands,
for the waters to bow down,
O Daughter of the Sky,
prostrating to your wounds.


11 **on the banks of waiting**

The ship's face is the face of all refugees,
and our face
is still searching the sky for the blockade.
The face of the sun was floating
as it faded away
and disappeared.
I swallowed the fire, the fruit of winter
but did not get full.
I stole what my life wanted
while death slept.


12 **a detail**

My mother
will draw our face in the sea in many colors.
She will feed the fish's screaming a picture of us together,

she will tell the days.
"This is my laughter,
and the water will mold me into a prophet
My talisman: Mother, Mama, a thousand Moms—the voice of
my four boys
I set sail on the pain of men, and I have no sails."


13     **waiting**

I will wait for peace,
I will sing every song I know
on the shores
to the water.
Women's secrets end at the seashore.
O Sea, wait for the whole story,
and don't ask questions
My mother is in your hands
so tell her,
"Smile,
and I will laugh
such that my features turn to rain
and your face becomes a spike of grain."


14     **a supplication**

Fatma readies for herself a path beginning at the end of her sea.
O Goddess of the Sea,
fill the water's skin with the seeds of your fear
and plant a garden in the sea.
Your woman splits her waters with water towards you,
so create dry land.

Don't think that the songs could be a mat.
Consider instead that if the water keeps flowing,
the embryos will commit suicide.

O Goddess of the Sea,
watch out
for the blasphemy of ships that go aground,
watch out,
don't send the coast guard like lying prophets,
for they spread water over water
so that land gets farther away.
Send me news like your light,
separate the sky and the water of your wave
and rejoice.
Your sea has narrowed,
rejoice,
your throne has narrowed.
The more cramped it gets, the wider the story will be for those
whom this life loves
and the less that can be held to account. The fewer gusts in the
breeze,
the wider the waters, the tighter the escapees' breath.
They accuse the foam at port of lying,
"There is no Goddess beneath the sea."

## 15    in the sea's grip

Fatma will be saved.
"I did not sin against the country, but the country sinned
against me,"
she says, continuing

"The wars of men, all men, have won, words have been
defeated, and the pilgrims are floating, circumambulating
the sea. This is the only path I can create."
She will be saved,
how could she not?
The sea fears her impulses
and dreads the love of salt on her moist mouth.
It will never believe she feared it
The waters know her disobedience
and the torrent of Damascene tears.


16      **the shore**

I am getting closer to the water's edge.
I stretch my eyes towards a shore I cannot see.
I pull what my wounds reach.
Here I am denying the impossibility of connecting dry land
with dry land,
Don Quixotely-seeking to bring together two continents.
There is a bridge over my chest,
and a train runs over me.
Down below, the boats lie at rest.
I hold fast, I wait, I cannot breathe, I'll meet my end
O Fatma's face, will you not appear?


17      **a maze**

Face to face
I don't see her and she doesn't see me.
I have become a sea.
My flesh is missing its salt.

I have become a bridge,
about to fall apart, and my bones are brittle.
O Face, come to my body and take a stroll,
War has closed the windows on the new,
and our normal part has gone
so that everything is now completely normal.
You alone
make normal surprising!


18     **a confession of absence**

Mother, come here so I can tell you the truth.
I am not like you.
My features may resemble the past,
but everything has changed.
I've trampled all of my shadows to smithereens
and walked toward the light—
there is no light like that of love.
The path has dogged me,
so I started doing the opposite of what the guide said
and haven't yet arrived.
The forests bite at me,
and the trees surround me,
forcing me along the path.
I am fed up with police stations,
their features suffocate me,
the ranks, the badges,
and the uniforms,
no matter what color they are.
I am the side road whenever temptation opens the way.
I am not like you.

I have opened up belief
and started searching for its truth alone.
I want neither the trustworthy nor the truthful.
All I have is my poetry in a book
which is no  revelation,
just a song gone too far in contemplation.
I'm not like you.
The truth is that
I resembled your Levantine face in Amman.
It saved me for a long time.
Oh, excuse me if I've gone on too long,
for you've kept the poem from its story for a while


19      **a song**

And now, O Fatma, and my Wound,
Now, O my Mother, and my Salt,
on the forbidden expanse, a capital is sold off.
You didn't sin against the city.
We reap what destruction sowed in the heart of hearts,
still deluded by thoughts of a quick return.
Sing! Let the wastes fight against the wastes,
for there will not be light
as long as there is not darkness.
Patience will never wash off Fatma's face.


Cologne 2015

# in the sea's playground

*Translated by Levi Thompson*

I see the sea
as a borehole
without a lover's face, reflection,
or waist.
It sucks at the ends, like mud,
like death,
and even those who know the way don't know where it stops.

I see water as a solid
because I am scared of falling,
like a sandcastle fears vanishing, I am scared.
We've met our end more than once,
yet we don't know
who has put off death.

Looking for revenge, I searched for an origin, my origin,
I have never known God so I could thank Him!

Amman 2014

40

# pictures from exile

*Translated by Nida Awine*

The skies of exiles
are the books of hungry people,
nightmares of those who survived the sea, those we don't see!

The clouds of exiles
are the tales that those who could escape tell their children
when they grow up,
lists of the absent,
airplanes without fire,
left unseen.

The faces of exiles
Faces that don't look like friends,
or martyrs,
or those who raided us in the morning,
or those who cooked our flesh in the evening.

The faces of exiles
are faces for us to forget,
and we ran far away to forget.

We will open a door for God
so perhaps He might see us,
so perhaps He might do as He wills!

We, the birds of those who set us free and left.
We, the weepers for those who reached the end, and lay
down to rest.
We, for whom life has become impossible,
and who did not survive
shall count the air for you, the wind.

They ask about Damascus.
I deny the falling bunches of grapes.
I cry a lot,
without any tears.
I stay alone like a stalk of dewy grass
poor
like the last alley resounding with the last of the living
in the evening,
like the sound of birds in my grandfather's house
who took shelter in my ribs
from the wrath of the sky.

Here they ask about love,
my love
I rave with the sound of a faraway call to prayer.
I see every blond as a sea for my salt,
pulling her braids around iron bars.

I wail
like a sad dog
because the girl forgot him for a kiss,

and I travel the earth
from one woe to another.

I exhibit a film about my love affairs,
and I cry a lot about what I've done.
I return from my tears,
and I forget
as if tears are victory and consolation.

Here, they ask,
and how much they go on asking,
but they don't ask to know.
The question's meant to show they care,
they're masters of switching bodies,
but they're better at forgetting.

Women of exile,
even if they are your flesh and blood, are exile!

Cologne 2015

# i will not die

*Translated by Levi Thompson*

Like any two people, time was eating us up,
like any two people touched by a *jinn*.
Time spread a delicious table over skin drowned in illusion,
eating us, and we bowed down
like so . . .
The shadow doesn't hide the tale,
so a candle's evening was a coincidence,
and a crying cup spread with wine . . .
until the dawn of changing clothes, place, and
hunger's house . . .
we waited for our flesh . . .
Then one day we
realized that if we get hungry
we'll devour time.

I was getting older,
my young friend.
I became an ugly beast,
picking up the young ladies, the old, pretty girls, and
not-so-pretty ones . . .

I peeled their bodies,
but
I would be lying if I screamed, "I've known love!"
I was getting older
without noticing.
The mirrors got used to my madness
and agreed to go along with the trick.

This desert thrives within my face.
I'm no sculptor . . .
I wrote in the testament of a lover before me
and faked the ending,

"I will not die . . . I've got enough poetry to fight off the idea
of happy tales."

Like any two people,
exodus asked us, "Did your face appear to darkness?"
Of course — in love — we snatched some dark so we could
kill death.
We argued after that.
"I won't die," I announced,
"I must finish writing my catastrophe between the camp and
the newspaper."

I'm still getting older without noticing.
Your face is tiring,
and fear has thrown two sperms into the womb of my song!

I got closer
and said to give me some time.
"I won't die tomorrow. I'll draw the breast of my new song."

O Life, short like a palm tree.
They cut out a dream for her.
Why, when I look at the faces, their faces,
do I say,
"I don't seem old. They're all older now."
Even though we're the same age?
"I won't die today. My hands will save me so I can tousle
the hair of far-off Amman."

O Time, we chose you as our God,
and after that we hungered!
"I won't die now . . .
I died yesterday from an excess of life,
and the poem hid it all away."

# where did we come from?

*Translated by Levi Thompson*

It just so happened that you liked a woman
hanging down from paradise
stretching out an arm from fire.
It just so happened that you hung down like a blind lamp
without a light,
family,
or dream.
A secret rope extends from her hand
towards the neck,
your neck, I mean,
so hang down a bit more to be saved.

It just so happened that you fell down one summer day
into a river,
and Amsterdam ringed the river with pretty girls and
not-so-pretty ones
tits, tits, tits,
red-colored windows,
red-colored beauty,
pimps,

and smoke.
Red, red, and the river takes on color
as its lips turn red.
Behind the glass a woman who looks like me beckons.
She looks like you,
and she looks like us.
Us, the exiles, the kidnapped, those who have come
to have no mirrors.

The smell of sailors on the walls,
women's voices—I hear them,
the melody written for other voices does not hide them.
The square is pregnant
with the dust of soldiers who went to war one day and
came back dead.
The square is pregnant.
Murdered, murderers,
tourists in Arab clothes.
Murdered, murderers,
the river licked its lips,
and night made it prestigious once again.
The red rises to light up the summer night, it rises
and I . . .
am an exile with no mirror.

Behind the glass I see her, a lady who looks like me.
I know her, she knows me.
People cross us,
and I cross them.
Behind the glass, the past comes into view and beckons.
A lady hangs down from my heart,

dancing naked,

looking toward me.

My cheeks redden like the river.

She dances,

I dance.

She asks me, "Where did you come from?"

So I dance.

She asks me. I tremble like a branch.

I hang down.

The past pours out, and I wake up.

I see myself as a lady who looks like her.

I ask her,

"Where did you come from?"

The river flows,

the ships die,

the tourists are naked.

God's clouds redden, revealing a red nakedness,

hanging down,

dancing,

asking us, "Where did you come from?"

and Amsterdam prepares her laughter for the next day.

# ahmad's drowned shadow

*Translated by Levi Thompson*

"It's your name," they said.
The one who named you got lost.
The sea was stretching to the heights.
Heavy is the sorrow of his migration which drags
your father into the depths.
He forgets the color of his eyes, floats,
and forgets who is behind the wave.
He floats
and floats . . .
like so . . .
until he rests in the sky!

"It's your name," they said.
They shackled your eyes with colors and waited for you
until you completed the sea,
until you were completed with the water of your eyes.
How will you let them know about the drowned,
the ones who killed you behind the sea,
about the sea salt,
and how the place lost you?

The one who named you got lost,
the sea got lost,
the land got lost.
Arise
from where death rose up and be saved.
Now that the boats are sunk,
how can you float?
The straw died,
so give up your old corpse
and cry
so that this sea can be relieved of guilt for the crime.

"It's your name."
Where is your shadow?
Your shadow is lost at sea,
while you are exhibiting what you know about life.

Your shadow is lost.
How was it you wove the story of the dead again
after they died?
You were floating, circling among the wood-hard corpses
around you,
trying to understand what they said,
what they hinted at as death approached,
what they heard,
what they were,
what they became.
Perhaps your shadow got lost among them!

For you
the open air is translucence itself
and your sea and the sky become one.
Everything in the sea became
your face.
Everything in the wind,
your wave.
The sea chose you alone
to spread your throne over the waters.

"The sea is mine,"
you said to the wood.
My shadow falls over you . . .
Your shadow remained drowned
along with the name:
Ahmad.

# they seem like people

*Translated by Levi Thompson*

They don't worship fire,
but they carry warmth like an old song . . .

They don't worship the sun,
but they ask the light to remain friendly . . .

They don't worship God,
but they search for the truth . . .

They don't ride the sea; it rides them.
It throws them—stripped of their memories—far away,
wherever it likes.
Now we know that whoever threw his hands upon the seas
controls them
even after he has drowned.

They don't write poetry,
but they were born together
from bellies.

Parents practiced telling them stories about colors and
dreams over the borders of thin paper.

They don't rise up to the sky,
the land rises up beneath them
to become freed wings . . .

They don't shoot guns at weddings,
so we ask them, "Why?
How else can we send out two belts of laughter across the land?"
They dance, not answering out of respect for the music.

They don't seem like people,
earthly languages know them as gods,
and the lands of Allah deny them.
They deny them, leaving them barefoot.
They ask Allah to be free!

How often unsung songs denied them.
Songs are homes, like the mistresses who
sold off humanity for a god,
though they didn't how to reach him!

They don't seem like humans.
Humans walk across their blood,
hungry and unseen.
You can see them when they go after the bread
of their countries,

no sound heard from their women screaming,
no sound heard from the cannons that kill them,
but
you can hear them when they go on about politics,
ask about life,
or when they're left in a row of old prison cells.

# fireworks

*Translated by Levi Thompson*

Atomic bombs
lit up the sky of Cologne yesterday,
but they disappeared before coming back down to earth.
They disappeared, killing no one,
destroying nothing.
Maybe that's why the Arabs call them
"fiery games."

Fireworks
are proof that you can play with fire!

They were playing music with firecrackers
and clapping whenever a star exploded in the sky.
The sky was besieged by military helicopters,
each one equipped with an HD sniper scope,
but they didn't drop barrel bombs.
They just dropped some balloons.

No one tried to run away . . .
except for me.

# escape

*Translated by Levi Thompson*

The woman who brings you back to your teens
the woman who steals your sleep like a squadron of bombers
the woman who returns your astonishment to you from
the mouth of death,
who makes you shake with ecstasy as her breath draws near,
who makes you lose your abilities to madness,
leaving you stunned and contemplating her magic, like
a child seeing an amusement park for the first time.
To get drunk off this woman, you crossed two continents,
two prisons, and three countries.
Watch out or she might give you a nationality and become
a homeland for you!
Give her a little refugee
and get out of there!

# just as death is born without love

*Translated by Levi Thompson*

Just as death is born without love
just as war enters without a door
just as it's raining now without waiting
just as everything is found within itself
just as a survivor boils with guilt about what happened
to save him
just as a pool of water thirsts
just as death appears from its songs
just as war ends without an ending
just as wishes rain down like waiting
just as everything is small
just as a survivor kills the guilt about what happened in his life
just as a puddle of water becomes pregnant
just as I desire her
I prepare my heart to meet her

# so we left damascus

*Translated by Levi Thompson*

So we left Damascus the way you tear out a fingernail.
We were alone.
You, who were more than the sum of our sadness
We waited, alone, to hear the goodbyes
and the voices of the women sewing up the exiles' wound
with their sadness,
and we were alone.
The first of us was caught up in survival,
the last of us tired from the long morning,
and you, who once told me,
"Don't sleep if sadness expresses its grief,
and don't ask where those who travel to their sadness go,
and don't follow those who go to the most coveted lotus tree."
You who said "No" when fear cleaved open the door
to salvation.
You, who once told me,
"Don't be scared if we don't leave the country for ourselves.
Fear for those who remain alone.
We were once alone or perhaps we wouldn't be."

So we passed by here, my dear,
by the gas chamber,
by the soldiers' songs,
under a bomb that hasn't yet gotten over yesterday's
drunkenness,
by our sadness,
before those who count our breaths with bullets,
behind those who overindulge in their crying.
We waited a long time.
Like someone who desires wine from longing,
we squeezed out our sadness together just as people squeeze
sadness out of grapes by stomping on them.
We said, "Tomorrow God will stop being so childish.
Tomorrow He will be ashamed."
My dear, we waited a long time,
and longing brought us no wine.

So we were saved just as they write on our face.
We were saved together, so wait for me.
They say that we were saved.
I don't know if we survived.
I don't know if survival is making it to the others
just as I don't know if we ever left there, Damascus,
as the dead leave life,
just as I don't know if Damascus will leave us as we would like.
So we were saved like a bird says it escaped from the sky,
So we were saved like an eel is rescued from the water.
We were alone.
We were alone.
We were . . .

We were saved, and on shore with the others we turned
around and said,
"So, Damascus, we were saved."
We were alone, then we were split up and sent
wherever whoever was in charge wanted.
We told her what birds say in cages.
We told her what an eel would say when it has ended
up on land.
We said, "So we were saved, O Damascus,"
but she paid us no mind.

# the disappointment of a smile

*Translated by Levi Thompson*

The wind eats our flesh.
We got lost dragging dreams of life
and fainted over them . . .
The tears disguised in the fragrance of longing's rain
disavowed yesterday
and denied the iron that remained alive in our hands . . .

The cold is bitter . . .
and dawn alerts a stranger, calling out,
"The mother is an old maid"
and God . . . how often we've said He will smile.
The smile was disappointed, and He kept frowning!
We came here to cry.
The time for crying ran out,
and this eyelid remained on guard.

Time trains depression
and lying mirrors . . .

The grass is lined with mines of memory.
As for the one who saw us off,
how can he forget his friend?

I'm there living among friends.
Every day we say how much we miss each other
and remember all the times we've cried.
I'm determined to throw my pain into their open arms,
so I stumble . . .
I'm so alone when I'm there!

# the miserable land of acre

*Translated by Levi Thompson*

Is it because Acre didn't leave its sea and went far away,
or that a wave afraid of my grandfather's wall
has held fast to stay?

Tell Acre that I am an old stone.
History changed the color of its longing.
Acre will disown me
because fear has forced me to emigrate north.
How can she remember a lover who threw
an adolescence of longing
into the arms of an Acre that is not Acre?

The luxury of remembering
fills the distant cup,
so the countries of the sea are split up.
Two capitals,
two songs missing a breathless melody asking for my presence.

Acre will know me . . .
If the camp knew the face of my child in the cold
countries from behind the wall.

Distance is a map for troublesome people.
I am like a piece of rusted metal.
My air is heavy with the dew of a coastal morning.
I follow the tracks of yearning without the one who yearns.

I tried to imitate the city in the camp,
but I missed its sea,
so I made a fence from the women of daybreak,
and the siege broke.

I was certain of our migration, and you were not.
Here you are coming to the morning, with the fragrance
of a land I have not visited.
You carry the sea in your palm.
The water runs from it,
but the sea does not.
You ask for the camp . . .
You didn't pass by its many streets.
All the neighborhoods of the camp are a bridge
to a memory of civilization.
All the names in the camp are memories of countries
we haven't visited.
They saddled us with the legacy of a map and a giant key,
so remind me,
I've gotten rusty, and the waters of the journey
have worn me down.

Tell me again,
where is Acre as far as I go?
How can my grandfather's wall slumber while
the siege nips at my ankles?
I am candy-coated,
and the siege is a huge rat!

The country's flag is just a colored coffin now,
so I ask her,
"Might I now, in naked longing—if I were killed by your hand,
if I died—wear your old memories as a coat?"

Acre will disown me,
for she has many times forgotten to mention
her mole on the cheek of the document.
Remind her
that the walls of the city protected her,
but they did not protect me.
Cities without lovers are stones.

"I will not live without Acre. The quirk of talking
between us, the confession of seduction.
I will preserve the secret of every gull who flies.
The sea knows all the secrets of politics. Only
the sea can bear the besieged grief of women!"
"Will she remember me?"
"She will remember. Don't blame her . . . stasis is like
a disease for cities."
"I changed. I moved on. I lived in prison. I escaped
and could not forget . . ."

"Likewise, Acre follows you with every window which will
open, so hide in a gull's wing far from the borders of fire."

Tolerate me, Sea,
for I am froth and your wave is dry land!
This is an attempt to bring dynamism to stasis.
The sea lives in miserable lands!

Acre tries to joke with me,
sending a picture of each night
sometimes draped in swimsuits during summers of longing,
others in the empty arms of a bed.
Acre tries . . . oh, how she tries!
Iron on top of iron
builds the real separation fence.
How can I compose a door in the expanse of migrations
to adorn memory as a country and longing as a wedding ring?
"Now Acre will not withdraw her prison.
She becomes instead a country of hopeless land!"

"It's up to me to love you when you come like a bullet, and you
can pick the songs. Books fall in front of your face. Amulets
closed the two doors to interpretation and cleared the way for
return. If I lived, I would have to choose between waiting on
sadness and forgetting. If you came back from nonexistence, and
what comes to widows came to you, and I had what your face
has of homelands, I would have celebrated without candles."
"It's up to me to love you roughly; it's up to you to flutter
in my blood. It's up to me to blow up founts of money or
museum tickets. When the clouds break, when the country

breaks apart, the soldier will bear the scent of tears."
"I told you there would be a lot of tears."
"Don't be so sad."
"No!"
"So we parted."

What if I spoke to the river
and gave a man fishing there a revelation,
"Strike grief with thy staff."
And what if I walked on water?
The fortuneteller says,
"The poets shall go mad."
What if I told my children
their father died from looking at his wristwatch?
The fortuneteller said nothing.
What if the river told me about poets?
What if I told the river
about the mole on the chest of a girl eaten by loneliness,
about my face when I explain the miracles of war,
and when poetry comes to me
like a woman does?
"The river would go mad."
And what if I spoke to God?
"He would go mad."

And when you get rid of whoever he is
wash your lips of
the remnants of his poems,
and wipe your blood
from the collar of his shirt

and be sure
that when you say goodbye
it won't be during a vacation, a holiday, or some other occasion.
Give the farewell the right to transform the everyday
into
a carnival.

# the dance

*Translated by Levi Thompson*

The dance
is a war between yourself and autumn.
Did you ever know
that your body is not yours?

Take the end of the rhythm
and fall down
like a dying eagle.

Take your beginning
my friend.
In love, there is always one who asks and one who is asked,
and I say—
just like everyone—
that I am an angel . . .

so she will come to the angel's drunkenness
to ask you.

The poem's text is love's margin,
music at a funeral, songs of childhood.
Your rhythmic verse is your thick beard.
The body of the boat,
the half of you left at sea,
is making it light.


Which one of the tales hurried along the creation of rhymes?
Which poetry died
but was not destroyed
at the time of death?


Two suns melting in the cold of care.
Each tyrant prepares for eternal life,
counting your wounds,
counting for you . . .


Two suns melting in the cup of seductiveness,
every cup a completed creation as it fills up with dregs.
Not my cup.
Each flame follows iron tracks,
becoming fire.
When it gives life the spark of my fire,
how many autumns hide behind iron
stretching out toward us like a spiteful head?
My cup was waiting at our cupbearer's door
but . . .
he was enamored and poured forth for you.

Hey you! You, who are left behind before the cup is resurrected!
Come closer!
Why are you so stingy?

If you want to,
dance alone without a cup,
without a song or sun,
without a wedding party,
without any dawn beauty for you . . .
You have nothing!
You have nothing.

Amman 2014

# inability

*Translated by Levi Thompson*

Inability: handing the dew over to the wind.
The butchered seagull landed in the hyena's maw,
having never swooped down on a meal like an eagle does
did not try to see them from afar.
How small they seem.
Look at the mirage encircling them.

Inability: gunpowder moving without hope!
Rifle fire leads me to my end.
Every day, impotent men are conscripted
to the gallows without resistance.
Who still remembers the lies of heroes
in the face of annihilation?
Will we rise victorious in defeat,
or will the waste conquer us?

Inability: a childless mother cannot wail.
A child who did not try out a crocodile's emotions,
did not live life in our death,
and the crow never fucked him.

Inability:
an inability to write,
to read,
to scream,
to struggle with the rape of memory . . .
inability is giving in to justice in the hereafter!

Amman 2014

# what dark wants

*Translated by Levi Thompson*

The people in this story
are now being created in the east—
the land of your death—
so look out for the sound of goodbye.
Aren't you the one who chiseled a poem on the water's breast?
Take that, and drink your peace,
so you can see all the mourners dancing, waving
without hands or screams.

The sleeping ones see us,
and they see the cups of the land without drunks.
O Brown Face of Ours, in your absence asking,
"Did you hear?"
"Do we answer, 'We have heard . . . we have been
forgotten in the waste'?"

Two hundred people are missing from
the slide show of our memory.

I saw them slowly walking to the highest points,
bleeding out of our faces . . .
A metal-winged bird flew right through the fingers of loss,
eating away our faces' features on their bodies . . .
and Allah pours out what water He can . . .
"Is this the miracle of separation?"
And He does not answer!

"I'll die by suicide,"
I read in a lover's will,
and the sun runs its course towards what dark wants . . .
without longing . . .
There's nothing about the lands
to narrate.
To the west of exiles,
there's nothing new other than vegetables.
We sold wars to color our faces
with all the colors of nature,
and we assumed that
that crazy red,
the colors of rifles and smoke,
and the idea of flags,
and school clothes . . .
were outside the natural order.
We disagreed,
but we decided that what you knew
and what I assumed were both wrong.
Here's a stable life,
today is a thousand times a day.

I'm sorry that I won't live here for long.
There's no place to write about my torture
or longing for my country here.
I don't want to let the fire of revolution
go out.

I'm fed up with poetry.
Storytelling's just a way to record my name,
strewn about in the streets' nonsense
I've taken rhythms towards prose.
It made me kind of happy.
My grief and putting off death have become a song.
I'm fed up . . .
I want to give the poem what it wants.
Do I have to translate clouds now?
I read . . .
Everyone writes that he's like a moth
around the flame of its beloved.
Glory be to the first one who wrote something down!
Creator of Poets, tell me, why were they all moths
in search of a flame?
What will I write?
Before I give the poem something to say,
I have to kill all the moths just in case.
If I can't, I'll have to eliminate the word
"moth" from the dictionary,
if I can't . . .
I'll burn the old poetry along with the new
and go into seclusion . . .
I'll have to write down a lovers' alphabet on floor tiles.

The people in this story are our people.
Two hundred people missing, absent.
Fear has finished them off . . .
the planes are slow,
but death is fast.

Cologne 2015

# no. 2935

*Translated by Levi Thompson*

*I shrink down in the gas chamber.*
*There, while the voices follow me and take me to myself*
*blood lights up yesterday's wall, the military uniform shrinks;*
*the guard of death becomes a guard for sadness and the dead,*
*the lake shrinks with ashes and our shadow. Pistols shrink behind*
*display glass in museums . . .*

"Close to the place's memory of fire, the tyrant shrinks like
a plastic bag, history shrinks like a piece of scrap paper,
nationalisms shrink like shoes, the places shrink, the ruling
parties shrink, the electric fences shrink, the ovens shrink and
burn, beds shrink and wake up to abandonment, military badges
shrink like dirty jokes, the names of the murderers shrink, and
the dead spread out in the air the water the dirt the fields, on
the walls and in books . . . and in my blood."

*There, where forgetfulness is our master, memory holds us back*
*whenever we jump over grass or a swaying flower, there is the one*
*who filled up the place with his ashes so he could return once*
*again . . .*

"The screaming shrinks so it won't be blamed
for living like a parasite off of a commemorative
photo of the murderers' grandchildren.
The grandchildren of killers always get more
than the grandchildren of the killed."

*They hide here*
*They choke here*
*The fire that ate them up was lit here*
*A banquet for death prepared like a song here*
*The forests still live off of them here*
*The river gets drunk off of them here*
*Women's hair is woven into rugs here*
*and when my heart falls out of my hand*
*a sparrow flies off*
*like someone offering a sad greeting to those walking on tears*
*those who are tired of blood*
*of nostalgia for the city*
*or lovers' hands . . .*

"Tomorrow tourists will come
to buy flowers
expensive tickets
prints
and souvenirs
they will spend lots of money
the grandchildren of killers usually get more than the
grandchildren of the killed"

I am the woman who understands the language of seagulls, who
reads the sadness between their wings, a sadness imprinted on
the chest. Everyone else forgot its name, so they started calling
it "the heart."

I am the woman who was a gull sitting on the sand, regarding
her white companions until one of them approached to sit
beside her and regard his white companions.

The woman who pecks at the water's face, making ripples that
widen until they measure the waist of memory. Fish jump out
of them and fall back in. I am the woman who devours her
memory, forgets to forget it so it devours her until it gets fat.

I make clothes for the men who kill me, uniforms that make
them naked.

*"Zwei neun drei fünf"*[1]
"Present!"

Clothes with badges raising the value of those
who put them there. I am the woman who does
not want to be branded by a yellow badge, I . . .
My shadow is fear: whenever truck lights approach, it gets
scared and closes its eyes, making me into a human shield.

---

[1]    The numbers in German here (2935) were found on the forehead of Rihab al-Alawi (1989-
2013), a third-year civil engineering student who was tortured to death in 2013 in Bashar al-
Assad's prisons. Her picture, along with 55,000 other photos of Syrian detainees who met the
same fate, was smuggled out by a defector.

I am the woman who was a gull, she alone never ate a corpse,
human meat, or . . .
the one who lived off the banquet of her fear,
never getting lost in the desert,
never giving birth to a god,
never marrying a prophet

Who, when she loves, breathes through her skin, granting hours
to time, each one much longer than sixty minutes and much
shorter than life. She throws them on the bed like a wet towel
drowned in lust and shrunken into a goodbye.

I am the woman who went into the streets in a nightshirt,
coming out of a magician's sleeve
shaped like a bomb
then exploding . . .
in tears.

I see the convoys coming
they go in as people
they come out as ash
I lift your skin up from death
I write a poem then erase it with my fingertips
I draw a theme park
I light up a remote village
I tame a rural river
I wring out a sweaty mountain
I kiss my face in the mirror of your skin

I peel your waist
I make your skin a brown shroud
and I say,
"The grandchildren of killers may indeed get
more than the grandchildren of the killed"

*I choked in the gas chamber.*

I went, and I did not know the trains that took us to the camp.
They brought refugees from the Balkans to Germany.
I returned, and the days had eaten my language up
I was born on the way to death
I died, and I was born again, and I died
Wherever I was, there was war
In the coming generation
I will be a rock that does not go to war
and war won't come to it
Or perhaps . . . I will be a war
The ancient Arabs made war feminine and Allah masculine!
Hey, Allah!
If you were a man . . . I'd kill you!

Between Berlin and Auschwitz, 2017